Copyright MorningStar Publishers

All rights reserved. No part of this book may be reproduced without written permission of the copyright owner, except for the use of limited quotations for the purpose of book reviews.

The Wheel of the Year

Yule

Forward

This pamphlet will provide a good understanding of Yule, the second of the eight Festivals of the Wheel of the Year and the way it is celebrated. Each of the eight festival have been extracted from the guide book, 'The Wheel of the Year. A beginners guide to celebrating the traditional pagan festivals of the year.' New suggestions on your celebrations available only in these pamphlets have been added. If you are new to the Craft this selection of pamphlets will give you a solid base from where you can increase your understanding of the Craft and its many branches. For the more knowledgeable they will provide tried and tested ways to celebrate each of the eight Sabbats of the Wheel in a meaningful and fulfilling way other than in a formal Circle.

Included in each pamphlet are lists of correspondences, guided meditation, spells and seasonal activities linked to the festival. They have been crafted to resonate with the Influences of the season and are the result of many years of personal celebration of The Wheel. Although I have worked within a group, my true path lies as a Solitary. I have accordingly aimed this book primarily at the Solitary Practitioner.

These Festivals are ancient, there is no doubt about that, but today, out of necessity, we often find we need to bring them in line with the parameters of modern life. Some of the practices and activities which would otherwise be impractical I have made more accessible by suggesting alternatives to traditional methods. Many of us no longer have access to open hearths and giant bonfires for example, so I have offered the alternatives I have found equally effective.

Life could be perilous for our ancestors and each festival marked a stepping stone from one seasonal change to the next.

Most of us no longer depend on the observance of the seasons to survive but the Wheel continues to turn and in doing so it demonstrate the astounding power of nature and its relentless progress. It reveals to us a power beyond our control yet one we can tap into. A power which is in the hands of the Divine. It instils in us a sense of awe and gratitude. For most, this gratitude expresses itself in the desire both to show appreciation and use that cosmic power to enrich not only our own lives but the world around us.

My hope is that these pamphlets will put your feet on the path of self-empowerment and instil a deeper appreciation of the staggering power of nature and the latent yet accessible power both within and around you. The Craft is not a 'dot to dot, follow my lead and do as I say' doctrine. It is a map. When you know the map and where to find what it is you need you can follow your chosen paths to it. Don't be told 'this way or no way'. Accept guidance, learn the routes then find your own way by your own self-empowerment.

Blessed Be.

Introduction

For the purposes of this pamphlet we will be celebrating the Goddess as the Triple Goddess - Maiden, Mother and Crone, as worshipped since the 7th millennium BC. And her Consort, the Lord of the Greenwood, in two of his guises, the Oak King and the Holly King. He is a God of fertility, growth, death and rebirth.

I have suggested spells and activities at the times of the year when the seasonal influences are particularly sympathetic to that particular intent. I have also suggested that some activities be performed during your ritual. They do not have to be performed within a Sabbat Ritual; indeed there are those who believe the Sabbat Ritual is solely to celebrate the Sabbat not for personal spells and undertakings. If you choose to keep the Sabbat ritual exclusively for the Sabbat then the spells and activities can be performed separately or within an Esbat (Full Moon) Ritual but preferably while the Elemental Tides, the influences of the Sabbat, are still active. They are at their height from midday the day before until midday the day after the Sabbat. Before and after that time they slowly diminish until the adjoining Sabbat influences begin to take effect. I have provided lists of correspondences for this festival. Correspondences are the colours, gems, herbs, incense, etcetera that are in tune with the season, your spell or your ritual's intent. For ease of use, and to allow you to select an alternative if you do not have the suggested item, I have included correspondence tables. With this you can link colour, gem stone, incense etcetera to the season or your spell. These are not meant to be exhaustive lists. There are many other choices available and no doubt you will add your own as you go.

Try not to get caught up on having just the right items, place, time, colour or any other of the endless conditions you think you need before you cast your spell or perform your ritual. Much of the power of your workings comes from your intent. Remember the old adage that *'if it be not found within then it be not found without'*. The power starts with you, the rest are aids, enhancements and focus items. See what works for you. Make notes then adapt and make more notes. Record which activities you chose to perform, the results of these activities and your thoughts, or suggestions, on how you can improve on it next time. <u>There are workbooks available here which are specifically designed</u> to work with 'The Wheel of the Year. *A beginners guide to celebrating the traditional pagan festivals of the year'*. They are perfect for creating your own Book of Shadows. The term 'Book of Shadows' simply refers to a record of things past; a shadow of all the activities you have performed and their results. It is particularly useful in allowing your power to grow and develop from your past experiences. It gives you your own personal guidelines as to what works for you. We are all unique.

When practising the Craft there is one major rule you should observe. It is known as the Witches Rede, sometimes known as the Wiccan Rede ('Wicca' believed to be derived from the ancient word for 'witch');

'If it harm none, do as you will.'

In the most basic of terms it seems to be saying you are free to do whatever you like. Sounds great! But it is not a licence to do as you want; it is a warning. It is reminding you that you must harm no-one and no-thing. And not just in the practising of the Craft. It is a pointer to a way of life. A moment's thought will show you that it can be far more difficult to follow the Witches Rede than at first glance; everything you do affects something or someone somewhere. You will do well to observe the guidance of the Rede however if for no other reason than whatever you send out will come back to you sooner or later. In the Wheel of the Year what goes around, comes around.

The Wheel of the Year
A short history

Most of the Festivals, or Sabbats, date back to pre-Christian times and all are linked to the changing of the seasons. The festivals marked a time to pause and reflect on what had gone before and a time to prepare for what was to come. The ability to understand and prepare for the relentless changing of the weather and cycles of crops and animals was essential. With the festivals our ancestors celebrated endings and new beginnings; the end of the earth's dormant period and the return of fertility culminating in successful harvests; followed once more by the end of summer and the return of shorter days, cold weather and the conserving and gathering of strength for the winter.

Although the festivals are ancient and mark important events in the cycle of the year the first known introduction of the year as a wheel was given to us by Ross Nicholls in the 1950s. The Wheel of the Year demonstrates the cycle of birth, death and rebirth in its never-ending journey. As the Wheel turns the Circle of Life is represented by the eight Festivals. They are divided into four Greater and four Lesser Sabbats, alternating about six weeks apart. The four Greater Sabbats, also called the Cross-Quarters, are based on pre-Christian festivals and are known as Fire Festivals. They are held on fixed days of the year. The four Lesser Sabbats, also called the Quarters, are celebrated on the two Equinoxes and two Solstices and so are based on the position of the sun.

Within the four Lesser Sabbats the two Equinoxes are Ostara (also known as the Spring Equinox) and Mabon (the Winter Equinox). 'Equi' translated from Latin is 'equal'. While 'nox' is 'night' so 'equal night' referring to the equal number of hours of daylight and darkness. The Equinoxes are by default opposite each other on the Wheel of the Year.

The two Solstices are Litha and Yule. The word Solstice translates to 'sun standing'. It refers to the sun's position in the sky at its northernmost or southernmost extreme due to the tilt of the Earth's axis being most inclined toward or away from the sun. So it is a time when the apparent movement of the sun comes to a stop before reversing direction. So at Litha we have the longest day and at Yule we have the shortest day. Again the two Solstices are opposite each other on the Wheel. These four Festivals divide the Wheel into Quarters.

The four Cross Quarters or Fire FesDvals are the Greater Sabbats. They are pre-ChrisDan and are based on cycles of life:-

    Samhain; represents endings and beginnings.
    Imbolc; a quickening.
    Beltain; ferDlity.
    Lammas, also known as Lughnasadh; harvest.

    Each of these four Greater Sabbats is located midway between two Lesser Sabbats and at the turning points of the seasons. They cut across each quarter dividing the Wheel into eight parts. In this posiDon these Sabbats look back to what was and look forward to what is to come.
    It should be remembered that the eight fesDvals are attuned with the changing seasons of the year and so must change with where you are; the northern hemisphere being a direct opposite of the southern hemisphere. So though, for example, Beltain is celebrated on 1 May in the northern hemisphere, it is celebrated on 31 October in the southern hemisphere. I have given dates for both the northern and southern hemispheres. The southern hemisphere dates are in (brackets).

Festivals begin at sunset and last until the sunset of the next day.

Samhain - Greater Sabbat 31 October (1 May) - Root Harvest. Death and Rebirth. Communing with Ancestors. Cross Quarter. Fire Festival. Day of Power

Yule - Lesser Sabbat 20-21 December (21 June) - Winter Solstice. Return of the Oak King. Quarter. Longest night.

Imbolc - Greater Sabbat 1-2 February (2 August) - Purification. Quickening. Cross Quarter. Fire Festival. Day of Power.

Ostara - Lesser Sabbat 20-21 March (21 September) - Spring Equinox. Spring Goddess. Quarter. Equal day and night.

Beltain - Greater Sabbat 1 May (31 October) - Fertility. Cross

Quarter. Fire FesDval. Day of Power.

Litha - Lesser Sabbat 20-21 June (21 December) - Summer SolsDce. Return of the Holly King. Mid-summers Eve - offerings to the Fae. Quarter. Longest day.

Lammas - Greater Sabbat 1-2 August (2 February) - Bread Harvest. Cross Quarter. Fire fesDval. Day of Power.

Mabon - Lesser Sabbat 20-21 September (21 March) - Autumn Equinox, Vine Harvest. Quarter. Equal day and night.

Yule
20-21 December (21 June)

Yule is one of the lesser Sabbats. It is a Quarter day midway between Samhain and Imbolc. At the Winter Solstice the daylight is at its shortest. The Goddess is Crone while the God, still in the guise of Holly King relinquishes power to the re-born Oak King. The Oak King will see us through the cold winter days the Holly King has prepared for us while he slowly lengthens the days and prepares the land for spring and summer. The increasing sunlight will warm the earth over the coming months and awaken the life waiting to be reborn within her.

This turning point of the year has been celebrated for many, many centuries. For the Norse and Saxon Pagans it marked the beginning of the New Year. The ancient Roman festival of Saturnalia celebrated the Winter Solstice. The name Saturnalia comes from the Roman God, Saturn, who was the God of agriculture. The celebration could last for seven days during which time there was a public holiday. Homes were decorated with winter greenery and there was dancing and feasting and gift-giving to honour the Oak King as the re-born sun. Remind you of anything?

Christians have many other traditions around this time of the year that can be traced back to Pagan practices. Naming just a few we can start with tree decorating which may date as far back as the Druids. Druids saw evergreen trees as symbols of everlasting life and used branches as decoration to symbolise the undying strength of the sun. Or how about kissing under the mistletoe? Well, the Druids regarded mistletoe as a bringer of peace. Then there is the Norse myth involving Frigga, the Goddess of Love, and the murder of Her son, Balder, with an arrow made from mistletoe. When Balder was restored to life Frigga blessed the mistletoe by giving a kiss to anyone who passed beneath it.

And don't forget the Yule Log. Currently, it is usually a chocolate covered cake in the shape of a log. Or at best, a log of wood decorated with candles. But the original burning of the Yule Log was much more exciting. It was the highlight of the festival. It involved selecting a huge log of birch, oak, willow or holly, though there are some that say only ash will do. Whatever was chosen it ought to be taken from the householder's own land or given as a gift but never have been bought. Before being burnt it was decorated in greenery, had ale or cider poured over it then sprinkled with flour. The fire was kept burning for twelve days then, with great ceremony, the ashes were taken from the house. A small charred piece was carefully preserved for the year to protect the house and to be used to light next year's log.

It is the lucky few who can follow the tradition in the way our ancestors did but why not do it on a smaller scale. Find a suitable log and after flattening one side of it so it will stand, drill three holes in the top to hold candles. If used during a Ritual use two green and one red candle at the beginning of the ritual to represent the Holly King then change to two red and one green to symbolise the rebirth of the Oak King. Or use red, green and white to represent the season, or white, red and black for the Triple goddess etc. Decorate the log with greenery, red and gold bows, seasonal flowers or cloves. Then dust with flour (before lighting the candles). Use it to decorate your Altar. If you choose you can burn your Yule Log in a chiminea or fire basket in the garden at the end of the ritual. If you are burning a Yule Log then save some of the ash for prosperity spells and the witch's prosperity bottle which I have included at Lammas.

Most Pagans will find that celebrating Yule coincides with taking part in Christmas celebrations to some degree; it is a rare pagan that has no Christian relatives. We may not follow each other's beliefs but the Joy and Love and Promise of this time of year is at the heart of both. And that is something we can all celebrate.

The Yule Altar

When decorating your Altar choose an Altar cloth and candles in a combination of red, green, gold, white and/or silver. Use sprigs of evergreen, holly-wreaths, mistletoe, clove-studded oranges and gold pillar-candles to decorate Altar and home.

Suggested Activities for Yule

Wild Bird Food

Wildlife needs all the help it can get at this time of the year. Put strings of cranberries and sunflower seeds out for the birds. Or make lard cakes for them using the following recipe.

1lb lard or suet, 2lb of a mixture of seeds, oats, chopped nuts, chopped dried fruit and small flakes of cheese. Melt the lard/suet and stir in the mixture. Pack into half coconut shells or mould it in shallow cups or soufflé bowls or similar and put to set.

Making a Wreath

Make a wreath for the door with evergreen, red and green ribbons, holly berries and pinecones dusted in glitter. Remove your decoration from the house after the Twelfth Night but save some in a corner of the garden to burn at Imbolc at the beginning of February.

Consider keeping a bough or bush of holly close to the door all year round as it invites prosperity into the house.

Seasonal Food for Your Yule Feast

For your feast choose from fruits such as apples, pears and nuts and dried fruit including plum pudding and fruitcake. For the meat if you are having any choose from turkey, game and pork. Choose a rich, red drink and perhaps some apple and cinnamon biscuits for the wine and cakes at the end of your ritual if you are having one.

Yule Correspondences

<u>Crystals and Gems:</u> The crystals and gems associated with Yule are the dark rich colours of lapis-lazuli, darkest purple-hued amethyst, emerald, darkest jade. Also quartz and diamond and all red gemstones particularly ruby and garnet.
<u>Element:</u> Fire/air
<u>Incense:</u> Frankincense, myrrh, rosemary, cinnamon,
<u>Flora</u>: Holly, oak, mistletoe and all evergreens.
<u>Herbs</u>: Sage, ginger, camomile, bayberry.
<u>Tree</u>: Holly.
<u>Colours</u>: Gold, red, green, white, silver and purple.
<u>Animals</u>: The wren is used as a symbol of the Holly King. While the robin represents the Oak King. Also Bull, Reindeer Stag and Squirrel,
<u>Tarot Card</u> - The Hermit: Representing the Holly King. Seeking enlightenment, wisdom.

Spells and Magical workings for Yule

Spell workings would ideally be for peace, harmony, love and new beginnings; things you are planning for the future; things you began setting the seeds for at Samhain or want to initiate now. Although the tide of the Wheel is ideal for these spells right now, real life is not that well organised. They can of course be performed at any time of need.

<u>A Spell for Peace in the World</u>
This spell is best performed at 10 pm as this is the healing hour.
It is a simple spell and requires nothing more than a white candle. It is best performed at your outdoor Altar if you have one or in a sheltered spot. Of course you will have to brave the cold and stop the candle from blowing out! Or you can sit before your indoor Altar and, as usual, try to ensure you won't be disturbed. If you are inside then put the lights out and leave only candlelight if you can.
Light the candle and look into its flame. Visualise the light growing brighter and whiter as it spreads out from where you sit. Charge its pure white light with the ability to heal and calm.
Repeat the following three times;

May peace prevail on Earth. (These words are the World Peace Organisation's pray.)

When you are ready blow the candle out with the intent of blowing this light into the world to do its work. Trust that the Earth Spirits know just where to send it and how to use it now you have charged it with love and caring.

*****

<u>Spell for a Safe Return of a Loved One</u>
A spell for the safe return of a loved one can be as simple as throwing a handful of grain after your child (unseen by her) as she leaves for school while reciting a few carefully chosen words such as;

Grain protect and keep her from harm

Bring her back safe to my arms.

*****

Or if someone you love is going away on a more extended trip you can do something more elaborate.

Spell for Safe Journey and Safe Return
You will need:
Three bay leaves.
A sprig of sage.
A piece of ginger or nugget of dried ginger or a pinch of ground ginger.
A small black pouch or cloth to wrap them in.
A white or black spell (small) candle. A short candle is best but if you only have a larger candle then you can put a small mark or pin a short way down it and burn it down to there. (Remember your magic sprigs from your intent, not your equipment.) Save the remainder of the candle for a safe return spell in the future.
A black pen and white paper, or if you can then a white pencil/crayon and black paper.
A length of black thread or embroidery floss to tie the cloth.
A pre-practiced sigil designed from a simple message such as 'safe return'. There is a sigil wheel with instructions for use in part three of this book. For those who are reading this in eBook format or simply would like a full-size sigil I have put a downloadable sigil on my blog at; http://maureen-murrish.blogspot.co.uk/

Arrange the items on your altar. Light the candle then make yourself comfortable on the floor before your altar.
Draw the sigil you have previously practiced and as you do so see the sigil being infused with the white light of your intent.
Open the pouch or cloth and put the sigil into it. Then add the herbs one by one and as you do so chant;

I ask Bay to protect you from harm.
And Ginger to warm you heart with my love.
I ask Sage to empower this charm
For a safe return to our home.
Tie the thread around the bunched cloth or neck of the pouch and

say,
As I will so mote it be.

Put the charm on the Altar next to the candle and allow the candle to burn out or down to the decided marker. Then the charm can be slipped into your loved-one's bag or pocket to take with them. When they return safely you can bury the pouch in a flower patch or put it into the recycling as a gift to the elements.

Yule Meditation

There is a guide to preparing for meditation in part three of this book. Put some quiet music on for background. Put a glass of fruit juice and some cakes or a favourite snack on a table nearby with your Book of Shadows or journal. Heat some essential oil perhaps frankincense or myrrh or burn some incense; camomile, ginger or sage or a combination of the three. Light a red (for the return of the Oak king) (or white) candle, or if you have a Yule log, light two green and one red candle. Have two red and one spare green candle nearby.

Close your eyes and begin your mediation in the usual way with deep breaths and active relaxation. When you are ready visualize yourself in a dark place. You feel safe and secure. Visualize yourself lighting a white candle then settle yourself down in the circle of light and look about you. As your eyes become accustomed to the dark you see you are in a forest of holly trees. Notice their shape, the outline of the branches and pointed leaves against the starlit sky. The old holly trees hold no threat. They look tired and ready to sleep. When you are comfortable with your surroundings think about the goals you hold most dear, the ones you plan to achieve in the coming months. Hold them in your hands like a tiny infant. See them grow strong and healthy. Imagine your ultimate goal achieved and feel what that will be like. Hold onto the feeling.

A ray of light touches your eyes and you look up. Through the old holly trees' branches you see the sun beginning to rise over the hills. As the light touches them the old holly trees change into young oaks. The sun touches your skin and warms it. Sit in silence for a few minutes and absorb the warmth and the feelings of achievement and success. Welcome the return of the sun with his promise of life, the fulfilment of dreams and the new beginnings he brings with him. When you are ready open your eyes and return to the room you are sitting in.

Give yourself a few minutes to return fully then snuff out the two green candles and replace them with two red ones to welcome the re-born Oak King as you say,

'The Oak King has returned and with him he brings the sun and new beginnings.'

Snuff out the
 red candle and replace it with the spare green candle and say,
'The Holly King has retired but we hold him in our hearts with love and gratitude until his return.'
As you eat your snack and drink your fruit juice or cup of tea reflect on the return of the Oak King and the never ending turning of the Wheel. Then write down any insights you gained during your meditation and how it felt to achieve all your goals.

Yule

Tarot Spread

1. How am I seen, what represents me?
2. What needs to be addressed and finished?
3. What am I ready to manifest?
4. What gifts should I draw upon to help me?
5. What can I expect between Yule and Imbolc?
6. What message does the Aged Goddess have for me?

Cinnamon Oatmeal Cookies

Ingredients

1 ¼ cups (177g) all-purpose flour (scoop and level to measure)
1 ¼ cups (120g) rolled old fashioned oats
1 tsp ground cinnamon
½ tsp baking soda
¼ tsp salt
½ cup (113g) unsalted buÓer, softened
¾ cup (160g) packed light brown sugar
1 large egg
1 tsp vanilla extract
1 cup (120g) finely chopped peeled Granny Smith apple (1/4-inch cubes or smaller)
2 tsp fresh lemon juice

Method

1. Preheat oven to 350 degrees. Line two 18 by 13-inch baking sheets with silicone baking mats or parchment paper.
2. In a mixing bowl whisk together flour, oats, cinnamon, baking soda and salt for 20 seconds, set aside.
3. In the bowl of an electric stand mixer fitted with the paddle aÓachment cream together butter and brown sugar unDl combined. Mix in egg and vanilla extract.
4. Toss apples with lemon juice in a small bowl. Add flour mixture to egg and vanilla mixture and mix unDl combined, then mix in apples.
5. Scoop dough out using a medium cookie scoop, or 2 Tbsp at a Dme, and drop onto prepared baking sheets spacing cookies 2-inches apart. Flatten them just slightly.
6. Bake one sheet at a Dme in preheated oven unDl cookies are set, about 14 - 15 minutes.
7. Let cool on baking sheet several minutes then transfer to a wire rack to cool completely. Store cookies in an airDght container.

Recipe source Cookingclassy

Herb Pouch

Sacred Space

This is a herb recipe to prepare the place you use for rituals or mediaDon. Hang it in the area and before your ritual walk with it three Dmes deosil (clockwise) around the space. Tie the herbs in a violet coloured cloth Ded up with a silver and gold cord.

When preparing these recipes chose a Dme when you are calm and not likely to be interrupted. Perhaps after a meditaDon or on a soothing walk in the garden or countryside. If you are using fresh ingredients perhaps you might be lucky enough to be able to collect the majority of them while on your walk. As always, concentrate on the purpose you are collecDng them.

- 2 Jasmine petals/flowers dried or fresh
- 2 rose petals dried or fresh
- 2 sprigs of rosemary dried or fresh
- 1 bay leaf dried or fresh
- 1 cinnamon sDck
- 1 pinch of rock-salt

- Tie the ingredients in a violet coloured cloth secured with a silver and gold thread hand hang it in your sacred space.

Other books by M Murrish:-
Work books:
The Wheel of the Year: *A beginners guide to celebrating the traditional pagan festivals of the seasons.*

The Wheel of the Year: *A 1yr 3yr or 5 year work book and Journal for the pagan festivals. (Companion workbook to: A beginners guide to celebrating the traditional pagan festivals of the seasons.)*

Three Card Spread Tarot Journal: *Ideas for three card spreads including prompts with room for your detailed interpretation and outcome.*

I AM....: *A prompted motivational affirmation journal to increase self-esteem and self empowerment*

Family Tree Research Journal: *Family history fill-in charts and research forms in a handy and logically ordered workbook*

Weaving Project Planner and Journal: *Designed for the beginner or experienced weaver working on a rigid heddle, 4 or 8 shaft loom.*

Gardening Journal Monthly Planner: *Organise your garden week by week with detailed record sheets and a diary based log book.*

Novels:
The Bonding Crystal: *book one of the Dragon World Series. A fantasy adventure with dragons, sorcery, elves and goblins.*

The Missing Link: *book two of the Dragon World Series.*

The Forth Gate: *book three of the Dragon World Series.*

The Lost Sorcerer: *A novella*

Thank you for choosing this Journal. If you find it as useful and inspiring as we do please consider leaving a posiDve review on Amazon as it will help others to find it too.

Scan the QR code below to check out our other books, notebooks, journals and reference books.

hi ps://maureenmurrish.com